Poetically **Correct**

BY

KIM MATTEAR

For information contact ;
www.goldenpublishingllc.com
goldenpub23@gmail.com
T : 754.801.3383

Book Cover and Title Page design by Michelle Phillips of
CHELLD3 3D VISUALIZATION AND DESIGN

ISBN :
979-8-218-02833-6 (paperback)

First Edition : August 2022

10 9 8 7 6 5 4 3 2 1

I DEDICATE THIS BOOK to my late mother and father, Cherryl & Leroy Mattear. They would love this moment just as much as I do right now. You are the reason I can do all it is that I do. Dad did always say, "You gone be just like your Momma"! Well, I do get it from my Momma. We are the life of the party. She would've been celebrating her birthday on the day of the book's release. I think of you every day. Now I can read my books in dedication to you. I still thank God to this day for both of you. You are both tremendously missed. I love you!

CONTENTS

PREFACE

EVERYONE HAS A STORY. We all have the knowledge to share and gifts to show the world. Poems are like lovely songs and adventures written in ways only the composer chooses. They can be deep, romantic, mysterious, serious, witty, dark, lively, and more. Poems can also include figures, family, and other people that have touched our lives. One of the most spoken persons in this writing is Kim's late mother, Cheryl. She was Kim's inspiration in how she loved children and demanded that they have a full life of enjoyment. She was loving, funny, soft-spoken, and serious about how children were treated. I believe my friend gets it now as she reflects on the ups and downs of life and what her parents taught her. They're no longer around to correct her wrongs and to reassure her rights. She has finally come to terms with it all, as her life took a turn where it all began to resonate. It is so wonderful to see Kim bring our childhood dreams of being writers and artists to books for others to enjoy. I'm honored to be part of this and can't wait for her to be part of mine! Within this work of art, the reader will find joy, laughter, and insight into the life and loved ones of my beautiful and gifted friend Kim.

Gesele McGlothin-Muhammad
Sister/Best-friend

Kim Mattear

1

You're a Star

You know you shine wherever you go!
People want to know who you are.
They see you're not afraid.

You're the spotlight on that stage.
Your teachers love the fact that you do it all.
They want you to be a part of everything.

You write, you play sports, love to sing, act, dance.
You're a star, you're going to go far.
I know you will, don't ever stop, keep going.

POETICALLY CORRECT

You're always involved in something.
You own that stage, you were born for this.
Your dad knows it's something special in you too.

You think he takes you to Hollywood
to audition for nothing?
Just as he make sure he's at every basketball game.
He himself knows if you keep going,
you're headed for fame.

It was always something about you,
that's how I know you're a star.
Hollywood is tough you know,
that's why I leave that up to your daddy.
Y'all won't get up there with me and get lost,
I won't hear the end of his mouth.

You know I don't care about children
making it in Hollywood at such young age.
You see these childhood stars around here,
that's exactly why I send your Daddy.
To make sure y'all have discipline,
you already think you grown; not that grown.

Uh-uh I really want you to make it on your own,
you got it in you.

You're a star,
everybody knows you are you stay at the top of the class.
You don't miss a beat;
can you leave something for someone else?

I know you love it don't you,
I can see it written all over your face.
Since preschool you'd sing
The Star Spangle Banner so loud and proud.
Singing the National Anthem every day;
prayer was still in the schools back then.

You don't wait on your friends
when it's time to go on that stage.
You have star power, that is your power;
be you don't let nobody change you.
I want you to be your authentic self,
I didn't raise no dummies or no phonies.

You make a mark in this world;
I don't care what everybody else is doing.
You keep your eyes on the prize, you hear me?
Be you and the hell what everybody else is doing
or you won't be no star!

2

Anything

Nice to Say?

Be careful what you say and put into the universe.
Don't think because it hasn't happened yet,
things do reverse.

Well,
I'm your mother and I tell you what to do, hear me?
So don't say anything
unless you got something nice to say.

It's not good just sitting around
looking for things to say about people.

That's not how we do things around here,
don't fool around blocking your blessings.
If you don't take nothing seriously,
you better take God seriously.
Okay, you think you cute if you want to,
God don't like ugly.

Damn right, God don't like ugly
and He's not very fond of pretty.
Don't listen to what those children say
about sticks and stones breaking bones.

Trust me,
when not being nice, words can hurt you
and stab worse than a knife.
Wounds from stick and stones
will heal before brutal words of the tongue will.

Words can mentally destroy someone's life
if they are not strong enough.
Yes, only the strong survive;
regardless of the fact, everybody has feelings.

The wrong words can emotionally scar someone for life.
You ever heard the saying, "hurt people, hurt people"?
Well, it's true and I don't ever want that to be you.

POETICALLY CORRECT

It takes more out of you
than add to your growth or real maturity level.

More importantly,
it defines your moral standards with God.
You don't want to be
putting the wrong messages in the universe.

When karma comes back around,
that witch hurts to get back what you've done.
It's just best if you don't have anything nice to say,
just don't say anything at all.

Those same friends you trying to impress
will use it right back against you.
There's nothing wrong with having common courtesy
in treating others how you want to be treated.

You should never have to demand your respect,
and you shouldn't have to ask.
No one should ever have to beg you to be respected,
respect is due to a dog.
Moms said to respect the janitor
the same way I respect the CEO.
Never assume you know
someone's ambition or next move.

Cause all that does is make an ass out of you.
It takes a moment to lose everything,
that one work so hard for.
Don't let it go to your head now;
shrink it down some.

I don't care how much money, cars, or clothes;
makes you no better than anyone.
You need to buy something worth something,
owning up something.
That's when you got something,
you know how many cars your daddy bought me.

You think I give a damn cause
people talking when they see me walking?
I laugh because I make the decision
to walk wherever it is I want to go.
I tell y'all all the time don't stop walking
now just because you have a car.
Don't get lazy being dependent on things
you have to all the time.

People can think what they like,
you don't owe anyone anything and vice versa.
Let them think and wonder, for all their dear life,
that's time they don't value.

POETICALLY CORRECT

Who they are and what they do
has nothing to do with you, unless you want it to!
Be mindful of the company you keep
and be mindful of what you say.

You can be aggressive too.
Be mindful of how you say things.
Don't make it a habit of saying things
to people just to be liked or accepted.
You can't be yourself like that,
you'll always be looking up to others' expectations.
Set your own stage, don't be a follower either.
Just be you, the best version of yourself;
you can't be anyone else.

You may find some people that want to be like you,
 they can never be you.
Be you and all you can be
and don't be nasty towards people.
The least you can do is be nice,
With something nice to say, or say nothing at all.

3

You, Me and She

I didn't know her; she didn't know me.
Two total strangers soon to meet and greet.
Neither one of them knows what soon will be.
Me, looking back now, I'm flabbergasted in awe.
She surprised the hell out of me.
Seemingly, seems to all the time.
The first merry-go-round was overwhelming.
Surprisingly, might I add, in such good ways.
Feeling like weight had lifted off me.
By any means necessary, vowed to follow my dreams.
Connections binding business aspects into projects.
Like Cardi and Offset, we want our own private jet.
On and off set, we make progress.
I happen to meet a sister who was seeking success.
That's how it ended up with you, me, and she.

POETICALLY CORRECT

She didn't run all this by me.
I mean, she really didn't have to, after all.
She took me under her spreader wings.
She took me in inspiration, I accepted in admiration.
Our color code black and gold is the color of our blood.
The blood that represents our love from where it grew.
Who knew she would be what she is today?
Who knew she was golden?
Who knew golden would be more than just a color?
She is definitely golden; hear me when I say she golden.
Her calm and cheery voice, smiling through the airwaves.
Positive energy floating around, she say, "hey now!"

Queens do real things like Super Cindy screams.
Queens don't compete! That would be she.
You, me, and she, we represent the Queens.
We rock like the Queens we are with our Kings.
Not holding down, we lift each other up.
On two different sides of the map.
Many of us, Covid was out to catch.
Leaving some of our loved ones never to breathe again.
Changing so many lives for the worst.
During these trying times, we sought what was best.
Instead of giving up, we gave it a shot.
They say a shot a day may kill Covid.
Giving it a shot before I ever decide to take that shot.

During trying times, I'll give it a try.

You only get one shot at life.

She gave it a shot; I gave it a shot.

You and her best friend gave it a shot.

I took my shot coming to the windy city.

Knowing I don't do the cold.

One thing they say about success if you really want it,

You have to do a lot of things you don't want to.

When it comes to success, do what it takes to get there.

She did her part, and she became an LLC.

With her best friend right beside her.

She brought in the new She R.I.F.F in town.

We couldn't do it without you either, cause see, She Sassy!

Brought along the golden girl, you know She Golden…

Sisters in company, we are family.

From the Midwest to the east, we are S.H.E.!

She brought along He, now that makes, you, me, and She.

4

Dainty

You always exclaimed to me exactly how she'd be. Dainty, soft spoken like you; unlike me. Feminine, skin-in skin-out, femininity without a doubt. Feminine, productive, power doll in love with self.

You said it, she is all that, one of my names from way back. In deep thought thinking of you and her Nana too, who knew? Tall like you, sounds like you, with certain gestures too. I catch it here and there, *"mmmHmm"* oh how it reminds me of you!

Independent like you taught me to be is she. One of the greatest feelings, when I see you living through her. Constantly reminding her, you knew exactly how she'd be. She's tough like me and handles matters like a champ!

She wakes up like a champion every day. Just like you always said, "You know what to do"! I don't have to remind her of what she needs to do. I didn't ever have to wake her up to go to school. I've not ever once had to tell her to get up get out and get something.

When it comes to her, it's all or nothing; she goes for it all. She's the girly girl you knew she'd be, that you were always looking for in me. Dainty she is, she gets it from you and her Nana, not from me!

5

My Brother's Keeper

Always made it my business to be the big sister,
I'm supposed to be to you.

Your existence changed my life forever
and that's the God's honest truth.

I'm always here for you,
I'm doing it for you, and my daughter too.

No matter how old or gray we get,
I got you and your 3-kids.

Children, I like to say,
we are all God's children.

14

I put that on everything, I got you.
Nobody needs to put you on.

My loyalty lies with you in whatever you want to pursue.

Before I had my child, I lived for you,
now both of you.

Both of you are my reasons why I strive like I do.

The hell with people
they may say one thing and do another.

I love you to pieces and thank
God every day for you Brother.

I pray for you every night before I go to sleep.

I cherish you forever my brother.

Am I my brother's keeper?

I pray God keeps me with him all his days.

I am my brother's keeper!

6

Gee

Friends since way back then at the age of ten. Named after her mom who got my ears pierced again at age 12. We're aging like fine wine, gone with the wind.

Gee-Bee is what I call her short for G-Baby. It sounds like an unfinished statement; see we have unfinished business. Unfinished business there's no pretending focused on winning.

Haven't ever denied me support or sold yourself short. We live different lives on different paths, our friendship is no disguise. What lies there is true love, genuine care and concern for one another.

From spiritually to politically we discuss it all.
No guy has ever come between us, we grew up like one of
the guys in some eyes. A child at heart when it comes to
laughter and our sense of humor.

Outspoken cause our voices will be heard spreading what
needs to be heard. She reaches out with open arms, need
no alarm as to what all is going on. Her good deeds only
knew a dear friend needed you.

That's been our vibe and that's how we do, since grade
school. Thank you for being a friend, you only question
my well-being and my needs. Your only answer is you will
always be here for me.

Likewise, Gee, friendship, sisterhood, we are family.
Thank you for constantly always reminding me. You
stood the test of times that I've been tested. Without
question, allowing me to learn my own lessons.

Always confessing your love and concern for me to do
better. Expressing in depth through mail sent, prayers,
phone calls and text messages. You will find a way to
reach out and offer your blessings.

Uplifted and gifted sharing your gifts with not only me,

but the world around you. I thank you friend for there's no other like you. I thank God for you, I trust you with my life.

You're such a positive light, you're right there when I need you. You don't ask me why I need it; you ask me when I need it by. You don't judge me; you may judge the result of the circumstance.

I know you're no saint nor do you wish to be looked as one. I can give you constructive feedback too and we still be cool. It's no one way street, truth seeks, and truth speaks. Your sanctification is upholding the Nation, royalty in it's making.

You are a living testimony; you are a part of my testimony. Neither of us are phonies nor of the fake phony bologna. We're loners, not ever lonely; facts, Aries to be exact. We stand on different grounds and come to far to turn back now.

We have so much in common that we share a common ground. We connect on so many levels, you need a shovel to dig it up. When I forget who I am, you are there to remind me. No matter the low points in my life you stuck by my side.

A brighter light shines upon your breed of four seeds.
You still managed to be there for me, when my Goddies
depend on you daily. I appreciate the love and support
from you no matter what.

No ifs, ands, or buts about it; this here can't be bought.
You're there whenever I need a friend doing whatever it is
you can. Thank you, Gee-Bee, for being a sister and a
friend.

7

Honey, Please!

Honey please, I don't want to hear nothing about no children. I don't get involved in with what children have going on.

They better mind they own, and not be found in mine.
I don't talk, or do any kind of business around children.
What business do they have; no business at all.

So don't you discuss any of my business in front of
children. You know what goes on in my house stays in
my house anyway.

Let me find out somebody went talking outside my house. That's going to be they sorry ass, that's what's wrong with folks now!

They bet not bring they ass back over here and I mean it. Don't let me catch none of them crumb snatchers over here again.

I will kick they ass myself, here what I say now; ole snake! Look, you can't tell me nothing about children, okay! A child is going to be a child, these children fight and be right back friends again.

Now who's the adult here, you or them? Well, you need to act like the adult you are before I treat you like a child. Honey please, have a seat!

8

Fuck Cancer

Asbestos crept through the passageways.
Creeping through my dad's body while at work.
Looking forward to World Way every day,
asbestos took him away.

Losing him left our family lost, broken, and lonely. Cancer you've destroyed so many families in various ways.

Killing souls at a rate meeting death at the finish line faster than a NASCAR race. The rate in which you confiscate lives at a spiraling, alarming rate.

The anguish and the pain so excruciating, I hate it.
I just wish my dad could be here for his buddy "Jake the Snake"!

He gave us all nicknames; we love and miss him to this very day. Fuck you cancer, for you are a silent creep that comes maliciously. A terrible threat like a thief in the night taking innocent lives.

Wounding families forever, thank God for the fight against mutation. Often taking our loved ones throughout the nation. We are thankful for the studies as well as the months celebrated in awareness.

Throughout the days, weeks, months, and years so many diagnosed. Many are faced to endure this, facing the fact they may be taken away by this. Cancer, you will not and cannot take everybody under. The best of luck to all who have been spared, cancer still sucks!

9

Get Out

Oh no
you won't walk in my house
without knocking.

Get out now,
then you may re-enter;
I don't know who you think you are!

Now you can come
in like you got some sense,
I don't care who take offense.

This is my house;
my husband pays the bills here,
who do you think you are?

Ok now!
You better get right or get out;
I don't care, take your children with you!

Y'all don't run me
or nothing over here,
this is my house.

You don't like it;
you can get the hell out;
the door is right there for you.

You
can let yourself out
before I put you out.

Oh,
you must not know,
I put little children out too honey.

Uh,
you better ask
these little children around here.

I do not play;
ask them do I play, they'll tell you.

POETICALLY CORRECT

They better stay sitting
they ass down somewhere
and watch T.V.!

I already fed them all,
they should be good
and ready to-go-to-bed.

Now don't you come up in here
disturbing the peace,
before I put you out.

These children
were fine before y'all
brought y'all loud asses in here.

If you wake them up,
they will be leaving
out of here with you.

Don't ask me to babysit,
then come in here
waking up my children.

What is wrong with you;
oh, you think I'm playing; get out!

Get your ass out of here now,

uh,

don't make me get up!

10

Malady Heart

Heart beats,
blood bleed,
heart ache,
heart break.

Heart chambers,
heart breaker,
more heart,
heartless.

Heart to heart,
follow your heart;
a righteous heart
is good to follow.

An ill heart may cause an ill mind,
heart disease is so unkind.
Attack the hearts of women
who are more accessible
and not as strong as a man.

We love hard enduring
heart-breaking moments
one after the other.

So much can weigh on the heart,
women are keener to the disease.
Heart disease is hereditary,
Yes, it can be very scary.

Our hearts are even bigger
so much weight on it,
but we can't wait on it.

We must
take better care of our hearts
now while given the chance.

Controlling our emotions
not to get the best of us.

POETICALLY CORRECT

Women birth the world
and receive not enough credit
for all we do.

Women
are mother nature's best friend
in relation to one another.

Thyroid
the disease that claimed
the life of my Mommy.

So now I must be careful
to watch for it
because it can come for me.

I claim not that it will not,
may God stop any harm
from coming my way.

Heart disease has no disclaimer on my life.
In God we trust, in Jesus name I pray.

1 1 Good News

There's no good new like God news.

The most resourceful of all.

Glorification at it's best.

No media tops this coverage.

Covered for life, life coverage for free.

There's a price for all us to pay.

Make way for all Godly things.

Natural born sinners continue to pray.

It's the God in me.

He's all in me, Creator of all.

In Jesus name, praise the holy spirit.

His only Son died for you and me.

In holy matrimony, highly favored.

What God does for me; He will do for you.

Which makes it impossible for Him to be selfish.

What God does for you;

He will do for me, as well as others.

He is a jealous God not an unfair one.

Good news right!

Good news is always good to hear.

POETICALLY CORRECT

Take the good with the bad.

Always look for the good in the bad.

Good news travels fast, bad news travels faster.

You knew? Who knew you seek for a prosperous future?

Watch your back, don't put yourself on the back burner.

Keep your burners lit, live in good ways.

Good ways will take care of you.

Good will always bring good with a grain of salt.

No fault with salty folks, not sweet.

The good news is God is good.

All the time, God is good.

What news is better than God knews.

12 Cheers to Joy

Life of the party let's get it started!
Fire and desire, taking life a little higher.
Nothing like the real love from you.

Missing your hugs, no shrugs, just genuine love.
Arms stretched out wide as the sea.
Miss you blowing kisses at me.
Blown so softly and gently, as well as your yell.

God forbid you ever had to call for help.
Just smiled myself, so courageous and confident.
In your own skin so cute. Nobody did it like you do.

Making life look so easy, like a smooth,
cool, breeze in the night.
Lights out, pipe it down, up for nights.
Day light again, oh joy came in!

Joy is welcome anytime. You know her?
If you don't know joy, you need to find her in time.

POETICALLY CORRECT

She waits on no one, anytime is a fine time for her.

Here's to all hear ye and listen well...

Don't let nobody steal your joy!

13

Soul Glow

Soul Glow everybody looked forward to daily.
So much love would be cooking on the stove.
Much love you've shown to many,
not for show though.

POETICALLY CORRECT

Flowing through life in the name of love.
Chin up, shoulders poised, head up high.
Thoroughbred, cornbread-fed, head brainiac.
Red head, red bone, long legs, light on your feet.

Walking and talking to your own beat.
Mile for mile with the most beautiful smile.
Full of life, becoming his wife straight out of high school.
How cool of you two to do, the cool in you two.

His firm demeanor, who dressed cleaner than him?
His cologne alone left behind such a rich fragrance.
The best man who could give examples of manhood.
The best of mankind in my eyes.

No nonsense guy, looking for him when finding mine.
My first date, the first man I was ever crazy about.
I owe it to the souls that's allowed me to grow.
Allowing your memory to live on in ways to help me grow.

You two were of souls
that had a glow only the Knower knows.
Getting answers through your nonexistence here on earth.
Oh boy! How bad it hurts sometimes; I won't deny.

Sometimes,
the tears of joy and gratitude are running down.
I'm so grateful God chose you to make my soul glow.

Your passings reflect the close holiday seasons
Independence Day and Christmas Day reminds me!
Standing for independence with Santa Claus to all.
Staying encouraged healthy and open minded.

Dreams continued to follow sustaining sanity.
Allowing the good to get the best of me.
Making sure the bad brings out the best in me.
We are spirits with souls forever lived,
that'll forever glow.

14

Thoughts

Creating the life, you want to live is not surreal!

Thoughts to the best life affirmed in due time.

Mind over matter, does even it matter?

Ever gave it any thought?

Just like love, it can't be bought.

A mind of one's own requires self-control.

As I think back, it's gotten a little better you know.

Sole controller, control your soul.

Spirits up high, flesh down low.

Pressure exuberates wild thoughts.

Don't let it fall to the wayside.

Terrible thing to waste the mind.

In race with time, winner at the finish line.

Address the thought process as it progress.

Nevertheless, trust the process.

Access the situation, more or less.
Yes! No sacrifice, no success.
Where I wanna be foreseen.
I dare you to believe where you wanna be.
Believing condition your thoughts to see.
Be your thoughts, live your dream.
Signs of your dreams in the making.
Every little step taken, is a big thing.
Patterned thoughts, planning thoughts.
Not exactly how I planned it, be it God's plan.
Not as I thought, more like I saw.
Coming to light; it shall come to past.
Father of all man has the whole world in His hand.
Take heed, nothing ever last forever.
Patience is a virtue, think to grow.
Stop, think, analyze; arrange, plan, execute.

Buckle up those boots, you're a hot pursuit.
Think pink, you wear it so cute.
Relevant thoughts of have knots.
Your next move can be for you or destroy you.
Just might be the one you can't say no to.
Think wisely prior for consequences may dire.
The one opportunity yet, you should've said yes to!
Thinking back to yourself... boy was I a fool!
Think wise if that means thinking twice.

POETICALLY CORRECT

Think wise even if that means wait a little while.

Just wait a while, nature knows the course.

Be mindful in your birthday suit.

Passionate thoughts of fire and desire are acquired.

Birthday behavior, highly favored!

Celebrate every day like cake day!

No gloomy day will take my shine away.

No time to play, much time for fun.

Get the job done, errands to run.

Mind constantly roaming with thoughts.

Just like love, it can't be bought.

You think you're the right one, wrong!

I've been there before that's for sure.

You are what you think, thought I knew too.

Thought I had it all together until I lost it all.

The thought of still having a strong mind.

No lost when it takes you to lose to win.

Things that make you go hmmmm!

You must want it to achieve it, as I thought!

Give it thought, you will begin to see it.

When you see, you can believe.

When you start to believe, nothing can stop you.

Not even the thought of giving up.

Give that thought no option!

15

No Pity Parties

For Me

You don't get it do you?

A poor as excuse just won't do!
Don't pity me, I pity the fool.
Pity me, I feel sorry for you.
I don't do pity parties, sucks for you.

I party like a rock star.
I rock wherever by far.
All by myself I rock like a concert.
I'm like an afterparty no shame in my game.

POETICALLY CORRECT

Ask me again and I'll tell you the same.
Put some respect on my name.
It's not all the about the money.
It's not all about the fame.

I'm destined to make myself a household name.
Don't pity me; don't judge me either.
When you fall; you must get back up.

Those who underestimate you,
don't know you well enough.
I'm far from sorry,
please don't feel sorry for me.

Folks wrote me off a long time ago.
What they don't know, unlike yourself; I take note.
Not to fight fire with fire just as long as my God know.
Be happy for me that I'm still breathing.

Calling me everything but the child of God.
The black sheep that would be me, ole heathen.
In constant prayer with my God
taking all my problems to Him.

Look down on me if you want to
God takes care of babies and fools.

Sorry you know, not me dear, I feel sorry for you.
When I die, I wish you not to be sorry for me.
Be happy you had to opportunity to have met me.

If I'd left if up to people to uplift me.
I'd already been left up shit creek.
Sorry is what sorry does, you even heard it from Forrest.
You believed him and not me
when you don't even know him.

Oh, cause I'm no celebrity, whose human just like me.
Sorry, not sorry, you are just too blind to see.
I'm not with any of your pity parties.

16

Roller Coaster

Ups and downs, falling now, scream and shout.

Hands in the air, waving them like there's no care.

Shaking goes the derriere, hair flying everywhere.

Riding out in the atmosphere.

Enjoying life, it feels good around here.

Who ever said it would be fair?

Loving myself with tender, loving, care.

Too strong to ever live in fear.

Kim Mattear

Too wise to know a janitor deserves respect like a CEO.

It's not always peaches and cream
on the other side you know!

Try very hard not to give in to
distractions or disturbances startling to the mind.

Forced to stomach it all in ways
that makes you want to regurgitate.

Rollercoasters are always an exciting venture,
not always fun.

Having fun and playing games, you don't always win,
just don't quit.

Like the McDonald's phrase, I'm loving it!

Every minute of every breath I take,
getting closer to my dreams.

Dreaming through the night,
I pray awakening leads the way.

Joy is coming, here she is another glorious day!

POETICALLY CORRECT

No complaints, no one is to blame.

Jesus, so grateful and very thankful
I call and praise your name.

Counting every lesson and all my blessings.

Took a big "L" and lost it all for the cause.

Like a freefall, sped fast; I fell before them all.

This fall hit the hardest, still I remained tall.

Stood in the paint, yet some days were faint.

Really able to see the real ones from the fake.

Paying attention to the little games people play.

Trusting my God, never losing faith.

He promised me His love will not ever go astray.

Life smacked the hell out of me with this setback.

So lost was trying to do everything for a strong comeback.

Focused so hard not to lose myself in the initial process.

Realizing I was lost completely trying to process this.

Lights shining on folks
how they deeply feel about me now.

True colors flying everywhere reassured and defining.

Refusing to except their treatment
beating me getting mad.

Not much family left for me
after the death of my mom and dad.

They taught me so much about life, I'm a survivor.

Yeah, it sounded all good at their funerals,
not that anybody lied.

Accepting the fact that I won't
be able to live this life without being tried.

I've been tried by people plenty of times.

I remember being that person on the other side.

POETICALLY CORRECT

I know and learn not to do unto others
what I wouldn't want for myself.

Folks love you when you got it all on the up and up.

They scatter with chatter box
mentality when you take that fall.

You're no longer a good use, they don't need you around.

You're no use to them, y'all use to be down.

Mama always reminded me, there'll be days like this.

Pay attention to the ones that dismiss you.

One day it's going to surprise the hell out of you.

Don't allow for them again to ever get that close to you.

They did it once, they'll damn sure do it again.

It will be your own family and so-called-friends.

People will snake you, the slime, the slick, the wicked.

Let that be that last time they trick you, far from a fool.

God will make them your footstool.

One day, they'll be in line purchasing tickets to see you.

It's okay we all play the fool sometime for the last time.

Before you know, you get hit with the bullshit.

Findings of what was once together,
split so quick, in a hot second.

So what, whomever it is, they're not even worth it.

If it means anything that's the end of the stick.

If the day circles back around,
they will see it for what it meant.

Sometimes that's what you get,
yet that doesn't have to be it.

From thoughts that roll off our tongues,
nothing goes unheard.

For every word spoken on down
to jokes and beautiful conversations.

POETICALLY CORRECT

We all go through some things; watch how you do things.
You never know who can pull strings
or will pull your string.

Always do from the heart, not for things in return.

Treat people as an equal addition to the matter.

For matters may subtract you too.

Expect the best of self and nothing less.

Be excepting of God's blessings and promises
He has for you!

17

Misery Don't Live Here

Mom said it best, misery loves company honey.

Misery don't live here, no will ill.

Quick, fast, and hurry, get it away from here.

Not in need of company that bad.

Bad company brings on bad situations.

Bad situations set you back.

Exactly what misery does. Fuck her!

POETICALLY CORRECT

She gets no credit from me.

She creeps like a thief in the night.

Lurking for grime time.

Trapped by the walls of deceit, I defeat.

You and your misery won't get me.

That company gets no parts of me.

The company you keep I care not to know.

Envy, jealousy, and misery owns no parts of me.

No certifications to cure this disease.

Self-love is the only pill to swallow.

Self-esteem boosts your health.

Don't ever compare yourself to others.

Self-doubt will leave you down in guilt.

You won't know what hit you.

Kim Mattear

Get to know joy, she comes every morning.

Channel your emotions around joy.

No one can steal joy unless you let it.

Joy makes us smile and cry through everything good.

Joy kills misery with kindness and common courtesy.

Bringing happy days even when we may be sad.

Joy can still be found during sad times.

It's not easy being happy when sad.

The state of being versus our feelings.

The matter in what are being not how you feel.

One of the reasons it's not good to be in your feelings.

Feelings are emotions that tend to change.

From situation-to-situation feelings may get involved.

This is where people tend to mess up.

53

POETICALLY CORRECT

They get caught up with jealousy, envy, and misery.

Majority of times; they either lie, steal, or cheat.

18 Love People for Who They Are Not *What They Are*

POETICALLY CORRECT

Many nationalities of the world tied to different religions.
Various types of cultures that exist in the world we live in.
Original and diverse origins whether domestic or foreign.
Adversities that reflect both you and me, plus everybody.
I know who and what I am, but what and who are you?

In due time,
getting to know one another will show us a thing or two.
Are you seriously trying to figure me out?
Ask me and I'll tell you?

Well,
how do you do on this beautiful day the Lord has made?
Are you glad in it, to see joy rising every morning in glory?
What you see is what you get, that's not the half of it.
You want respect?
You must give it to receive it. Got it!

Do you wish for people to like you for who you are?
What about those who like you for what you have?
Do you believe that's fair treatment?
What you think about people liking you
only for what you can do for them?

Same as folks dealing with you
cause of what benefits them.
No longer serving them a purpose,
after all they aren't worth it.
Don't get bent out of shape,
we were all brought up in different ways.

When people show you who they are;
that's the time to believe them.
Don't make up excuses
for them to continue hanging around.
Don't feel you are entitled to their judgement of you,
it's a reflection of them.

No more leeway,
make sure they stay on the road hitting the highway.
You may have dealt with them the long way before,
It's not like that anymore.
You can be the most genuine person on earth
and be taken for granted.

You can be the nicest person on earth
people still can't stand you.
You can be the grimiest person out here
and these streets will still love you.

POETICALLY CORRECT

So, tell me, do you want to be loved
or like for who you are or what you are?
Good question, when you don't have it all
or maybe even not the best-looking.

We come in different shades of color,
forms of shapes, with different styles.
Not all of us care enough
when it doesn't take much to even smile.
Like wow, how you like me now?
Only for what I was able to do for you.

Oh no, that aren't you,
I sure as hell hope not,
that's how souls rot.
I know I will not stoop down to your level
where there is no top.
I'd be a damn fool to give my shine
to a bloodsucker who cares not.

We are packaged in different sizes
blessed in assorted skin tones.
You know what they've said
about them red bones all along.

Kim Mattear

They also say the blacker the berry the sweeter the juice.
Sayings people base decisions on that make them feel
they're doing something.

Once you go black, you won't go back;
we stay hearing that!
We're all still short, stocky, fat, skinny,
boney, thin, slim, tall, slender, and chubby.

What qualities do you wish to see
in your wifey or your hubby?
Does it matter about hair texture,
or is it 'cause they from Texas?
Seen as attractive in person in September
as seen on the picture in December?

Personality!
Is there something in common or too good to be true?
Common courtesy beknows to,
sure it's always them and not once ever you?

There're always two sides to a story,
truth be the moral of it all.
Some just want to know it all,
with no wit at all, serving no purpose.

POETICALLY CORRECT

Know not your worth and value
but have the audacity to want to holler at you.
Ups and downs we all go through,
don't allow problems to get the best of you.

When you know your worth
and your value that's so powerful.
All the money in the world
wouldn't allow me to run back into your arms.

Free yourself from harm,
we all have emotions and realities faced with each day.
We all have a need to be sustained
in a place to stay in Jesus's name we pray.
We're all human beings simply trying to make a way,
some of us paved that way.

Some folks make it hard and difficult,
impossible for anyone to stay.
It's very important to know who you are as a person,
which is great for you!
Integrity you may know possessed in you lies good values.

Mom once told me, at times,
we don't realize we only have one foot in the door.
Thinking because we have it today, we need nothing more.

Don't ever get so comfortable in life where you become
heartless and effortless.
We are entitled to the decisions we choose
to make at the end of the day.
Think before you speak, pause before you act,
stop before it's too late.
We don't miss a good thing
until it's gone hoping it comes back our way.

My mother also told me,
what you have today can be gone tomorrow.
So, treat people with dignity and respect
for it can't be borrowed.
Love people for who they are, not what they are,
nor what they can do for you.

Stay true to your values and those worthy
of you, will value you.
Look for nothing in return,
always do from the bottom of your heart.
Warning signs and red flags we ignore from the very start.
Learn to protect your peace,
everyone doesn't deserve a piece of your heart.

19 I Don't Care

Who It Is

You are no better than anyone,
I don't care who you are or who it is!

God made all His children
equal the best sequel known to man.

He's not given any of us
that the other doesn't have when given life.

In life, He's given us choices and chances
to decide upon making the right choice.

It's not up to other people's standard
but yours to prove.

It's up to us to make the chance in making,
the right or best choice that's suitable.

We may not take the same route,
yet and still able to receive the same blessing.

No one is in comparison to God,
what He does for one, He will and can do for all.

While we are all made the same in our own little way.
Not all of us can go about it the same.

No matter how you look at it,
we are the same in His eyes.

He is always there when one wants
to make a choice to make it better.

Our character reflects the changes
and the choices we tend to make.

God loves you no matter what choice you make.
A difference in understanding when it comes to man.

Man will think he is better than you
and the next person for whatever reason.

Not only speaking of him, speaking of her too.
In God's eyes man equals man and woman.

POETICALLY CORRECT

We are different,
although we share differences in anatomy.

All require the same survival mode
of goals and means to live.

One is not ever too old
to be told right from wrong.

Whatever you do or wherever you may go,
just know you are not alone.

You will never be the only one,
let's get that through the skull now.

There will always be
someone better off than you.

With the same token,
there will always be someone worse off than you.

You must continue reminding yourself of
these things when going through it.

You are not alone and won't ever be!

Kim Mattear

Don't feel bad that you may be in a worse situation
than someone you may know.

That's the glory of it all in how you finish off,
set goals and execute.

There'll be times you have more than others, be a blessing.
It will not ever make you better than anyone else.

You can only be better
at competing with own life challenges.

I don't care who are and who it is,
you are not better than me or anybody!

20

They Talked About
Jesus Christ

Don't come telling me what somebody said about you!
You have to deal with these things for the rest of your life.
People are going to talk, let folks drive you crazy if you
want to.

Don't let that be you, believe who people show you they
are. So what people talking about you, they talked about
Jesus Christ. I don't care what people say, I care what they
do.

If they don't provide a roof over your head, feed you, clothe you, why worry? So why in the hell you telling me about what somebody said about you?

Have you ever thought you might be doing something they really like? No need in you trying to figure it out either! If you call them your friends, you need to find out what a real friend is.

Cause friends don't talk about you or talk down on you. A real friend has integrity and defends you when you are no where around. Not sure why else they would take time out of their day to discuss you.

They will see where it will get them sitting around talking about people. Those same fingers will point right back at them. Let them make an ass out of themselves and not you.

Don't let people like that change who you are, cause of who they are. So watch very close of who they are; everybody is not a friend. Get rid of them, even if family thinks they can do you any kind of way.

I tell you one thing; you will always have a friend in Jesus who loves you. All you need is God who created you, remember that honey! So, don't come running to me, telling me who said what about who.

Tell them, you don't care what they have to say about you. Let they ass know the reason why; 'cause they talk about Jesus Christ!

21

I Love My Life

I love God. I love me.
I love my life.
We're made in God's image.
It's the God in me.

POETICALLY CORRECT

I'm so grateful for my life.
So grateful for life itself.
Embracing the good with the bad.
Not such a bad thing, I say.
For real it's not.

Always finding myself laughing at the end of the storm.
Worrying use to get the best of me
until meeting worry not.

My whistle tone, "Don't worry, be happy".
Don't! Don't do it! Faith up!

Man up! Woman up! Love yourself!

Love your life! It's yours, nobody elses.
I love being me. Be you!

22

Relly

I call her Relly; we go back like the phone booth tele.
She really stepped up to the plate in my absence.
As I was trying to make some sense of it.

You filled in for me, when I needed you to help care for my
seed. While holding down your position at home with
your own family.

You were there for me when I couldn't be there for my
own. My dear friend, my heart longs for you and losing
your son. Apart of me was gone when I had your help
assisting me. Your son is no longer here with us, I know
not what that feels like.

POETICALLY CORRECT

What can I do for you friend? My question to you at the end of the day. I pray for your strength every day, asking peace to be still with you. The most speechless I've ever been in my life; I knew not what to say.

Seeking ways to reach out, I just flew out to be of support wanting to do more. But how? I still constantly ask myself. She would do it for me, she's done so already. She has done it for my daughter as her Godmother in her own right. Relly you were there for me and my daughter. You believed in me after all these years that've gone by. You invested in my dreams; words can't express the gratitude I have for you.

I thanked God for you then, I thank God for you now. Only God knows how you do it, only He know how we will get through it. Only God can get us through some of the things life has thrown at us. We were once young girls walking to and from school trying to be grown.

Happy we were coming into motherhood was exciting; yes, you were right there. You always showed how much you care. You always confirmed status and would just be there. Now I ask God, show me the way Lord how can I be there for my friend?

How can I show her how much I still appreciate her and what she's done for me? Sherril is her name; I had no idea she would step in and do what she did. I thank God for you loving me and my child unconditionally.

Marjon, God bless your soul; you have a Mommy that will always love you. She has a heart of gold. We love you too, may your soul rest in heavenly peace until again we meet.

23

If I Was a Boy

Will you close your legs,
remember you are a girl!

You are not a damn boy!
Well, stop acting like one!

Look how you're sitting in that chair;
girls don't sit that way.

You even sound like a boy,
you don't want to be a girl?

That deep voice comes
from your Daddy.

I'm right here, stop being so damn
loud hear; I hear you.

Do you have to act like a boy?
Maybe you should have been one!

What if I was a boy, Mama?
Sometimes I really think you should've been a boy.

When are you ever going to wear a dress?
Wear a dress sometimes besides going to church.

Don't ask me about getting a jerry curl no more,
letting your ear piercings close.

You'll really look like a
damn boy without earrings!

Obvious you like boys,
good I don't have to worry about that with your fast ass.

Confirmation with no hesitation,
Daddy waiting to give me an ass whooping.

Shooting basketball like my Daddy on the court,
name any other sport.

POETICALLY CORRECT

You should be tough on the girls' team,
you play just like one of the boys.

Aggressive, sweating my press n 'curls out,
hopping walls and fences every day.

Stay out of folk's yard,
Mr. John and his shotgun may not be so nice next time.

Fuchsia lipstick hit my lips in the
7th grade to take school pics.

Moms looked in awe when she saw,
looking with a glimpse of blush y'all.

She began to lay low with the
"you act like a boy" blows.

The girly was in me,
slowly but surely beginning to show.

Baby fat thick, hairstyle always
popping out with the feathers on 'em.

Levi and the guess store,
corduroys, and 501 denim blues.

Kim Mattear

Owning every brand name tennis shoe,
call me a sneaker freak.

Fresh from top to bottom from my head to my feet.

Spiffy in my cross cords with a tee or button down,
how ya like me now?

24

I Get It *Now*

There used to be no care in the world
when I was a little girl.

My parents always warned me
about wanting to be grown.

Wanting to be grown before
allowing myself time to grow.

I didn't know of course I didn't know;
hey I get it now.

I thought I wanted to be grown
until it kept growing on me.

Kim Mattear

Mom, you never told me anything wrong.
Dad, you were telling me all along.

I see now how important to you
it was for my sister and I not to fight.

Like a thief in the night,
the days back then reflect the times of today and now.

As you two are still very much a reflection of me,
I refuse to live in vain.

All I can do is look back there and
stare at what stares me in the face today.

I see where I went wrong,
it's not easy being strong without you.

God created me to break the chains,
generational and family curses.

Living out my purpose in pursuit
of my dreams as I continue to represent you.

My biggest supporters who did anything for me,
barely any that sits before me.

POETICALLY CORRECT

Dad, I understand the plan you had
and why you would get so darn mad.

Mom, I understand and
see now everything you said.

It all makes more sense to me now.
I'd be lying if I said it make sense.
I'm just making sense out of it.

25

Haute

Virgo

Oh, everyone could tell you
were a high-class fashionista!

Haute Virgo, the first black girl
I knew to work and hang out in Beverly Hills.

Wearing heels from junior high school
I should've knew.

My dear, darling you,
we bonded at your 12th birthday slumber party.

POETICALLY CORRECT

Me, you and Buttons kept the party
going playing hot toes, lol!

The best slumber party I slept to yet,
not long after we met.

Reconciliation facing us in our
early adulthood from being rubbed the wrong way.

Bumping into you at the
Century Club with a kiss.

We looking like twins,
had to get our picture taken that night.

Looking fashionably cute
as you always do sweet and petite.

Our bond grew even stronger
as we grew older with you being so discrete.

Could've surprised the hell out of me.
Damn it man, how I miss picking up the phone to call you.

Who ever knew the best
understanding would be coming from you?

Kim Mattear

Who else knew what I was going through but you?

Who knew that you and
I were facing the same exact thing?

Who knew Haute Virgo, who knew?

Who knew this was an initial
dedication to three dear friends?

Who knew that it'd end up
dedicated to only you?

Only we know what was
discussed during your last days.

Confirmation at its best, you passed the test.
Afterall none the less, I must contest.

Nevertheless, a dear friend to me if not one of the best!
We shared plenty memories and shared many secrets.
None of which has gotten back to me yet.

Being the loners,
we are trying not to put our problems onto others.

POETICALLY CORRECT

Finding our living situation without a roof or cover.
High achievers have not the perfect life either.

Taking on responsibilities for our little brothers.
Like the son you gave birth to, you would do anything for.

We still mourn you and one day will have to join you.
My dear lost friend I still adorn you.

On this new journey
I thought you'd be here with me.

My one and only volunteer,
seeking how to be there for me.

Literally wanted to sincerely help me further my career.

Your last days was so bittersweet,
didn't know you were leaving me.

You sent for me,
how could this be, who knew?

In so many words
I can only think you knew.

Your final words spoken unto me
basically, instructed me for what was coming.

I thank God you called me
the night you went to the hospital.

I would do it all over again
to spend your last days with you.

Watching "The Bobby DeBarge Story"
you manifested your funeral.

Telling me "Kim-Kim you better sing
at my funeral" like you knew.

I knew what song to sing,
you even spoke those words to me.

I couldn't imagine it the way you had the doctors
going to get you out of there.

You were ready to go home and
wasn't going out without a fight.

After talking to Zi, you,
Cassy and I cried that night.

POETICALLY CORRECT

God is the man we praise,
He has the last and final say.

It was close to Independence,
you and one of my mom's favorite holidays.

Speaking of independence,
I lost you both close to that day.

You were a very independent woman,
stubborn not looking to rely on a soul.

You ask me to do you a favor,
how could I leave when you sent for me.

I didn't want to leave you;
I didn't want you to leave.

The doctors were preparing for you to check out.
In the name of Jesus, God said come to me.

You began to exclaim how bad you wanted to go home.
I'm saying to myself, earth is not our home.

What home is she talking about?
Cause we both are out of a home.

There was no one else to think of
but our God to take you to the King.

Before the doctors could check you out that day,
God was preparing you before He called you home.

I found myself at your funeral singing
"Take Me to The King".

The first funeral I ever did sing.
Who knew Haute Virgo, who knew?

26

Today is a *Good Day*

H old up, wait a minute! Put some faith in it!
Today is a good day,
be great and give thanks.

Be joyful in your days,
longer days for you shall come.
Today is a great day, I will be great in it.
I choose joy, we need more joy in today's world.

Remind yourself that all things
can be done because you are great.
Great things happen
when comes to the mind, when you apply.
Let me get it straight,
let's straighten it out, aligning my chakras.

Kim Mattear

Motivated, yet never would've made it without Him.
Every day is a good day the Lord has made.
Every day the Lord is good making today not only good,
but great!

Jesus is the reason we have a chance
to wake up every day, give Him thanks.
The will of God is always good;
today is your day.
Make it a good day!

27

Stop Looking Ugly

You're not that cute!
God does not like ugly, and
He's not too fond of pretty either.
Sitting there frowning, that's so ugly!
You're too beautiful to be frowning.
You know looks will only get you so far.
You'll be scarred tomorrow with that look on your face.
Looks get old you know; they wear and tear.
You will not go anywhere with me looking like that!
Whatever it is, shouldn't mess up your day as such.
Messing your face up,
don't go around people looking like that!
Your face will be wrinkle before you know it.
Alright now,
keep on frowning your face gone stay like that.
That's so ugly…

28 P.A.R.N.E.L.L.

Prevent	(suicide)
Acts	(act now)
Related to	(depression)
Negligence	(is absence)
Evolve in	(get involved)
Life and	(be happy)
Love	(we will always love you)

29

RODNEY

I was happy to find out at age 11
that I had a blood brother from another mother.

Before my little brother came along,
I always longed for one.

Daddy loved us all,
I'm sure you knew that too.

I was so happy the day I met you,
they would compare me to you.

I played basketball like you and Daddy too,
I believe I told you. So did Jason too!

I was on a team back then playing
my position as point guard.

Kim Mattear

I see you made the newspaper in California,
just like Dad did in Florida in the 60's.

I always questioned whether
our dad had other children.

The year of 1987 brought it to
light one starry night.

Looking back now,
Daddy may have felt it was time to tell us.

Unknowingly at the time
he had just learned he had cancer.

I always asked the question;
he could no longer hide the answer.

Much respect to my mom,
she tried to tell us in so many ways.

She really left that up to him
to tell us in which they did together.

It was bittersweet, cause at the same time,
I wanted a brother.

I wanted you to be able to come visit us,

POETICALLY CORRECT

it was cool coming to Gardena.

I wanted a brother so bad;
I begged my mom to have our little brother Jason.

He was born that next year and
I've been crazy about him ever since.

It was also during the year
we met that I believe Dad was diagnosed with cancer.

However, we wouldn't learn until months
before his death just 7years later.

He told no one,
just like you had done before your death.

DNA is a serious factor I tell you,
I seen that when I saw me looking like you.

It was crazy at the same time amazing;
I would love to do it all again.

I know damn well that's not happening,
those days aren't ever coming back again.

No Dad told no one in the
household when cancer took its toll.

Kim Mattear

I saw something different in him and
called him out at my senior graduation.

I had never seen daddy walk so slow,
I walk fast as hell because of him to this day.

I'm like no way this is not the way my dad moves,
 no not at all.

So, when I learned about what had happened
to you my heart sank.

I was wondering what happened
to you since speaking to you last in 2014.

I would just pray all is well,
I wish you didn't hesitate to ever call again.

You had a sister who needed you;
you also had a friend in me.

Seeing you last since dad's funeral
didn't ever sit well with me.

It was out of my control,
so onto the memories I hold.

POETICALLY CORRECT

I pray that your children
and I can pick up the pieces down the line.

Daddy made sure to keep
his family together as much as possible.

Finally introducing you into your sisters,
we both resemble him.

I immediately saw it thinking
I was going to be as tall as you.

We both were dark-skinned like
our dad with our butt on our back.

That's how he developed the nickname
Aobb at Dillard High School.

The name means ass on your back,
I had it bad too with my baby fat growing up.

A little fun fact, I sure have his slim legs and
we were both athletic just like dad.

I just wonder now how your last days were spent;
I pray not in vain.

Kim Mattear

It was a blow to the face
to find out through google you no longer existed.

That news had me twisted,
asking God to fix it, how did we miss this.

All I have left is memories;
thankful for the few pictures I have of you.

God called you home,
no more pain and facing your fears alone.

We will always love and miss you Rodney,
may your soul rest in paradise.

Your memory lives on through us all,
wishing I could give heaven a call.

30

The Best Teacher

The process is real, trust it.

It flows with grace, face it.

The act of being, only for the moment.

Doing me only, not lonely.

Lately, what you do for me?

Allow life to, it will show you.

Just show up, don't ever give up.

What goes up, will come down.

No ups, no downs, 10-toes down all around.

Don't let up, get through, overcome.

It takes losing sometime to win.

Whatever it is, is already won.

Put your mind to it and just do it.

Walk your walk, actions speak louder.

What do you know?

Where did you grow?

We will never know it all.

Some talk a good game as if they do.

Don't be fooled, don't be cruel.

Judging books by the cover?

Cover your grounds, protect your surroundings.

Protect your peace, on the other side lays a beast.

Rise and defeat, no lies and deceit.

All eyes on me, all the way back to elementary.

School was cool, once it ruled.

Using God's tool; I got what I need and so do you.

Respect for my leaders and their teachings.

The best teacher we all know is evident.

Her name is Experience, don't you forget!

31

SHE & I

It was the sidewalk for me
Took me back to the old school.

Hopscotch traced in chalk scrolling pass.
Scrolling back with time like I been here before.

Seems so familiar, I used to do this.
Feeling like a big kid again.

I miss playing outside on the block.
Jump roping, double-dutch bus.

Kim Mattear

Take me back to a wonderful place.
A picture is worth more than a thousand words.

Going down a familiar road, unknown.
Interested in going, prechecking the path.

Something touched me in an instant.
No warning signs or red flags.

Occasionally requested information neglected.
Boy was I being tested, I confess it.

Mind positively, pondering productively.
She wasn't the one to object to my collaboration idea.

Kindness killed when she was almost
told to get the hell out of here.

The most humbling, warm, and gentle spirit is she.
The feeling of angels surrounding me.

Ignored change of heart,
immediately the journey starts.

Fears put aside, too good to be true.
Why would I believe what she saying to me?

POETICALLY CORRECT

Go with your gut and shut up sometimes.
One of the best decisions ever made in life.

Research finding similarities already.
Gold and black, alright now, this is where it's at.

The colors took me by surprise, like Mary J. Blige.
The connection felt so real then.

Reaching for my pen, I get the writing.
Playing catch up with memory taking note.

Like this is not a joke, I've inquired before.
Things don't always happen with the ones you know.

Sometimes it's better when a total stranger comes along.
The way things happened that day, it was meant to be.

It all came to pass and there was she.
She and I, now apart of each other's lives.

Two mindful sistah's with the write crime.
She just started the writing journey.

For years been searching for mines.
The connection went from awkward to genuine.

Now, Shenitha Finesse is one of my lifelong friends.

She and I are sisters in business 'til the end.

I am SHE!

32

No You Won't...

I Beg Your Pardon

We speak when we walk in this house,
no you won't, walking up in here.

Kim Mattear

Now you can walk back out my door
and come back in the correct way.

Or feel free to go back where you came from,
it's up to you.

I beg your pardon,
no one comes in my kitchen when I'm cooking.

No you won't question me in my house,
I didn't know you was the FBI!

I beg your pardon! Well, that's what you act like
questioning me in my house.

I don't know who you think you are,
no you won't!

I beg your pardon,
honey no you won't ask me to ask your daddy.

What's the problem with you asking him,
what you done did now?

Excuse me,
I don't get involved in situations that don't involve me.

POETICALLY CORRECT

I beg your pardon; I'm not telling anybody anything.
No you won't honey, try and be slick if you want to.

I don't take orders from people
cause my footsteps are not ordered by them.

I cook for my household,
so not many to take my order either.

I beg your pardon;
been living my life straight out of high school.

Me and my husband made sure to enjoy our marriage first
before having children.

No you won't,
ever put any of your children's' father on child support.

I beg your pardon, don't come to me crying over no man
that's not your husband.

Boyfriend's show you all the warning signs of him having
no plans on ever marrying you.

That's why you date, don't get caught up in all the titles of
being someone's girlfriend.

Kim Mattear

I beg your pardon,
that's what friends are for.

No you won't ask me to get up and do something you can
get up to do yourself.

If I wasn't here,
what would you have done then?

I beg your pardon, anyone living in this house
better have a job or be in school.

No you won't try to run game on me,
do you know who you talking too?

I don't see no fool but you,
you know you's an ole slimy, slick, and wicked!

Didn't I tell you my mother didn't raise no dummies,
believe me when I say.

I've not raised none either,
I beg your pardon, no you won't!

My husband takes care of home,
my girls are well taken care of.

POETICALLY CORRECT

He's crazy about our son,
he can do no wrong in his eyes.

No I won't sit and worry about children all day long,
concerned, yes!

They better choose to do right with the guidance and
morals provided to them.

I beg your pardon, of course I will always love you,
you're my children.

No you won't run my life either,
I beg your pardon.

I brought you in this world,
I will take you out; don't play with me little girl.

You think 21 is grown, you ain't seen grown yet;
wait until you on your own.

You'll be wishing to come back home,
no I won't be looking down crying about you.

I'll be in heaven saying, I told you so,
you don't listen with that hard-ass-head-of-yours.

Kim Mattear

Me and your daddy talk about it all the time,
I beg your pardon.

You damn right I told him,
now you have to deal with him.

I told your ass, you don't listen;
you'll listen next time won't you?

I told you I was gonna tell him,
no ma'am you won't have me looking like a lie.

I beg your pardon;
you better go in there and talk to him.

No I won't speak for nobody,
you better learn to speak up for yourself.

You in trouble now,
you might as well get it over with.

Regardless if I love you or not, your ass is hard-headed;
now go see what your daddy want.

"Will you stop calling her name like that,
she's coming; that's why she so damn loud now".

POETICALLY CORRECT

Hurry your ass up in there so he can be quiet;
your ass was walking fast when you left here.

You not walking fast no more, uh huh,
you thought I was gonna defend you this time.

I bet you won't leave me in the hot seat
with him no more 'cause you don't listen.

No you won't take advantage of the things I do for you,
just because you're my child.

You're not Jesus, and you sure as hell not God,
hell, you're not even my child; you're His child.

I just had you, that's just why
I will take you out; you came out of me.

Don't end up in nobody's jail, cause I'm not coming to see
ya or coming to get you out!

You better call your daddy;
you don't want to have to call him, do you?

Uh- huh, you know better, don't you?
You know how he is!

Well that's on you,
you'll learn next time, won't you?

Oh, I know you will, if there is a next time honey;
y'all won't run my pressure up!

If you're not dying,
I'm not coming to no hospitals either.

I already have to see that place when
I go to work every day.

I'll see you when you when they release you to go home.

I beg your pardon, children or not,
nobody's going to drive me crazy.

Not you, nobody! I beg your pardon honey,
no you won't!

Oh no you won't show your ass then call yourself getting
mad 'cause I read you.

Oh no you won't darling I beg your pardon,
honey you read wrong!

POETICALLY CORRECT

I don't know who taught you how to read,
don't go there again.

I don't mind teaching you a lesson,
you'll learn one way or another.

Kim Mattear

ABOUT THE AUTHOR

BORN TO THE late and great parents Leroy and Cherryl Mattear, Kim Mattear was delivered at Kaiser Hospital on Sunset Blvd. in Hollywood, California. She was the baby of the family to her sister until her little brother Jason was born. Kim admires him so much. She and her siblings also share an elder brother named Rodney Mattear (*not born to her mother*). Recently finding out early 2022, God called him home at the end of 2020.

Kim is the mother of a beautiful daughter named Kimyah, who will always be her pride and joy. Kim is determined to leave a legacy behind for her daughter, her brother Jason, their children, their children's children, and so on. Kim's heart had been set on making the world a better place long before she became a grown woman. She has the same vision now that she had back in the 1st grade during her first stage performance. Her vision from that day set a spark that made its mark on her.

Kim Mattear attended several schools in the Los Angeles County area with enriched honors. She has been in school settings since she was an infant at 8 months old at Thompson Learning Village. She attended a pre-school called "Kitty-Coo" for a year, soon to return where her schooling began. She went on to finish kindergarten, as her parents re-enrolled to attend a black-owned school, who were also friends of the family who owned Thompson's Learning Village. Graduating to grade school, she attended private school at St. Paul Catholic School. She attended the private school only for her first-grade year, where she also would become a Brownie of the Girl Scouts. That's when she began to explore her talents. She started public speaking, reciting written material, and singing at the tender age of 6. By this time, she was already fond of writing. After her demands to be removed from private school settings, she was afraid she would become an early school dropout too soon in her life. Her parents immediately considered the thought and followed up by enrolling Kim in public school.

After attending Arlington Heights Elementary School, Kim graduated, moving right next door to Mt. Vernon Junior High, now known as Johnnie L. Cochran Jr. Middle School, where she would graduate and attend high school. Attending valley school, she enrolled at Granada Hills High. Shortly after, she transferred to Dorsey High, where she would complete most of her high schooling. She would continue some of her high school education at Los Angeles High School and Crenshaw High School. Finally, returning to Dorsey High School and subsequently graduated from View Park High School.

Enrolled in Los Angeles Trade Technical Community College, Kim took advantage of the arts in modern dance music and the introduction to music. Lastly, Kim attended City College in Fort Lauderdale, FL., majoring in broadcasting. Although Kim holds no degree other than her high school diploma, she's received several accolades, trophies, medals, and prizes throughout her life. Kim is keeping her eye on the prize when it comes to her dreams and success.

Kim owned her very first business in 2012. Three businesses later, she now owns and operates *Be You Apparel Enterprise.* She looks forward to releasing her anticipated debut album one day soon through her music BMI music publishing, "Golden Life Music Publishing." Acting is also a big part of her life. The movie High Maintenance 3: The Stakeout is worth its wait. Expect to see so much more in store from Kim Mattear. Project Next L.A. is still her baby on the way!

Kim Mattear is honored to be a sister company under the umbrella of S.H.E. Publishing LLC. S.H.E. is optimistically growing businesses with fellow sister companies, R.I.F.F. Publishing LLC and The Sassy Enterprise LLC. As CEO & founder of Golden Publishing LLC, "Where the Art of Writing is Golden," Kim Mattear is ready to serve her mission. She often references the statement, 'We are family! I got all my sisters in S.H.E!"

POETICALLY CORRECT

Being the network marketing magnet, Kim is always networking. She is now involved with a new company as Coach Realady with Total Life Changes (TLC). Kim is seeking to relaunch her nonprofit for children very soon, which derives from her clothing line mentioned above. Writing, dancing, singing, and skating are her life. She expresses it all in her music. If it wasn't about love, that's what she would be writing about. Her passion for it and why she loves it so much led to her popularity at L.A. Trade Tech when her English teacher approached her about performing. The English professor told her, "No matter the writing assignment topic, you always find a way to talk about music and dancing!" Kim was asked to participate in a dance routine, except for being able to sing in the show, and she accepted the offer. She not only performed in the show: she provided the wardrobe. The group of ladies agreed on an idea for the song's performance. Because certain members would get stage fright, Kim found herself taking over the show. Kim's mother would let the entire audience know that her daughter was on stage, but that would be the last stage performance her mother would see.

With such a huge heart, Kim has a passion for helping others. Her journey is to seek her true purpose in life. Her friends and family expressed how proud they are of her, especially her brother, Jason. Her parents would be most proud of all. Her mother would be jumping for joy. Her father would be so happy with the biggest smile on his face. Both of her parents would be so supportive of her endeavors. Her Godmother Shirley would joyfully say, "That's our girl!" Her daughter's Nana (Barbara) would be there to support her with open arms as she always did. Kim loves and misses them dearly.

Kim Mattear

A message from the future best-selling author:
Passion is the force of quality that drives you.
Drive your passion to your destiny!

POETICALLY CORRECT

ACKNOWLEDGMENTS

I'M GRATEFUL TO GOD to whom I give thanks, thanks, and more thanks. I can't thank Him enough. I must say, writing this book took me on a spiritual journey with my mother. It wasn't sad at all like I thought it'd be. It felt like she was here talking to me. Yes, I cried once or twice, but not for long. She used to say not to cry when she dies, because she lived a good life. I found myself smiling and laughing so hard, reliving memorable moments. She was a live, high-energy person with positive vibes everyone wanted to be around. She meant well even when she was cursing you out. She was a joy to be around even when she wasn't. At the end of the day, you know Cheryl had a heart. She cooked big, she loved big, and she loved to be gathered with loved ones. That's what I miss so much. Real love from real ones and that she was. There's nothing about life and people my mother and father didn't tell me or try to inform me. I used to be able to talk to my mother about anything, no matter what it was. I enjoyed being around her; she had wit and was funny. My mom is real cool. She never really allowed anyone to get too comfortable with the thought of how cool she really was. Especially when it resulted down to children. She was real cool when you weren't on her bad side. She stayed ready to read somebody, giving you her reality check! She would always talk about how headstrong I was; sometimes, she thought I was too stubborn. I lightened up a little bit. At times, I think a little too much. So many fond memories.

The majority of the poems in this book reflect on the love and some memories of my mother I miss hearing, just as I can remember her do and say. She was a big ball of fire who enjoyed life to the fullest. My mother has a lot to do with who I am. She was my number one fan! My writings are something she and my dad was proud of. I want to continue to make them both proud!

Feel Free to Google Me:
@Kim Mattear and/or Realady
@goldenpublishingllc

Kim Mattear

SPECIAL THANKS

FIRST AND FOREMOST, I thank God and Jesus Christ for everything. I'm very grateful for His mercy, glory, grace, and favor. I am nothing without God. I thank my Mom and Dad for giving birth to me. I thank them for teaching me to be the best that I can be. I thank them for all they did, and all they would do if they were still here. I give thanks to my third-grade teacher Mr. Drummond; it wasn't just what he did. It's what he said. He wrote on my final report card of the 3rd grade, *"I hope to purchase one of your books from the bookstore one day."* To this day, I'm still grateful for his encouragement. It always stayed with me. It never left me.

I thank most of the teachers I had. They would always motivate and inform me of the qualities they'd seen in me. They recognized my good grades and the skills I possessed.

I also thank my daughter, Kimyah Henderson, for giving me a reason to live and leaving her a legacy for generations to learn about and fulfill. I'm also thankful to my little brother, Jason Mattear, for always believing in me and supporting me wherever, whenever, or however he can. I appreciate him for that! I thank my Godmother, Shirley Colquitt, for believing in me as well. She was another cheerleader, along with my Mom. I thank Lady Dice (C. Nicole Jackson) for being my support team in everything I do since becoming business partners with her. I've learned a lot from her in progressing in various industries of women in entrepreneurship pushing to break barriers.

I would also like to thank my childhood friend, my best friend Gesele Muhummad, for her everlasting support throughout the years, allowing me the peace in the right place to be, which made it possible for me to see this opportunity in the first place before my eyes. Finally, I give a warm thanks to Shenitha and the entire S.H.E. Publishing Team. I feel this experience was meant to be. I must personally thank Queen Shenitha for her welcoming me with open arms and extending more than just a service to me. I appreciate and thank her for her consideration and the tremendous amount of moral support she continuously offers. I thank any and everyone who has ever believed in me and continues to believe in me. I thank God for everything overall.